CONTENTS

Dedication

Copyright

Preface

Chapter 1: Swan Pond 1

Chapter 2: Intensity 2

Chapter 3: Prepare Yourself 6

Chapter 4: It starts… 15

Chapter 5: Virtual Reality 20

Chapter 6: Bad 28

Chapter 7: Take Responsibility 31

Chapter 8: Feelings Speak Louder Than Words 38

Chapter 9: Breakdown 41

Chapter 10: Fear is for Champions 43

Chapter 11: Mirror, Mirror 62

Chapter 12: We are Equals 67

Chapter 13: The Child Trick 73

Chapter 14: You Are Your Best Guide	76
Chapter 15: Put Yourself First	84
Chapter 16: Sleep	88
Chapter 17: Morning and Evening Routines	95
Chapter 18: Helpful Questions	105
Chapter 19: Zoning Out	108
Chapter 20: Make Peace with Your Purpose by Knowing Who You Are	112
Chapter 21: Wear the Cape	115
Chapter 22: The Manifesto	117
Chapter 23: Go Forth and Prosper	120

Special Thanks to:

YOU - for reading this and for doing the work to use your emotions for good. I'm so honored to have you on this journey with me. Kristen Seitz, without your photography, and your friendship, this dream wouldn't feel real. Thank you for taking the perfect cover shot. The Clueless reference in the book was for you! Lisa Arnold, for my back cover hero shot. Thanks of course to endless loving support from Aaron, Jordan, and my family - especially to my mom and dad for all those sleepless nights in my intense childhood. I'm so lucky to have such a loving and supportive family. Thank you to all my friends throughout the years who have stuck with me and supported me through my intense ups and downs. And finally, thank you Allison Melody, the Rise & Bloom Mastermind, and Laura Petersen. I wouldn't have committed to doing this if it weren't for you.

Copyright © 2019 Marisa Imon All rights reserved. No part of this book may be reproduced without permission from the publisher, except for use of brief passages quoting author

PREFACE
START HERE

I am not perfect.

I have daily struggles with my intense emotions.

But for the most part, I work *with* them and use my emotional intensity as a tool to help me live a better life. It feels like a superpower.

And I truly believe it is one.

The extreme ups and downs of living with bipolar type 1 took me to strange places in life - both literally and figuratively - and for awhile the only way I knew how to live was heavily medicated. Now I want to make it very clear right off the bat, I am not for or against medications - they saved my life on more than one occasion, but they also made life much more difficult for me on even more occasions. For now I've been living medication-free for the past few years and loving it. But who knows, that may change.

I'm not a licensed mental health professional, so

nothing in this is clinical advice - I'm just a human sharing my experience in hopes it will help. In hopes you won't feel so alone.

Instead of running away from or trying to numb the ups and downs, I now embrace them. I work *with* them. I use them to power me and the work I do. I use them as guidance. And they're awesome.

That's just it, intense emotions are awesome. And *you* are awesome for having them. Regardless of your medication choices. Just because for now I have been living happily medication-free, it doesn't mean medication is right or wrong for you. I was told by over a dozen mental health professionals that I'd have to be medicated for life and I wish I had evidence that there was another way, because to be honest, I never really liked how any of the multiple combinations of pills they gave me ever made me feel. That said, I know many people who do.

In the end we just need to do what's right for us, and I want to say this up front so that you don't get confused throughout the book and think that to do this you must be medication free like I currently am. That part truly doesn't matter and that's a very personal choice between you and your healthcare provider.

What *does* matter is that you have a gift: the ability to feel things very intensely.

What matters is that you use that gift for good.

Super Intense

This book is designed to show you how.

CHAPTER 1: SWAN POND

There I was. Cape whipping in the wind behind me. Swans circling in the pond below me.

I could feel the winds of destiny rising to lift me up and propel me into the hero I was born to be. There was much injustice in this world that needed correcting - with my hands on my hips I solemnly swore, "not on my watch."

△△△

Fifteen minutes later I was out cold in my bed.

Why?

Well...while the hero within me tried to stake her claim on saving the world, her arch nemesis got to her first...

CHAPTER 2: INTENSITY

My mom always says that when I was an infant, if you asked my dad one word to describe me, it would have been: "intense."

Now I don't remember too much from my infancy, just the general memories everyone has - crib-lying, thumb sucking, and finger holding, but apparently I still somehow made an impression of being intense.

Wait, what? You don't remember your infancy? So weird.

...Okay, fine, I don't either but if I did I assume those would have been the memories.

I mean, how can a baby be intense?

Now I think my dad would probably still use that word to describe me as a fully grown and (mostly) functioning adult.

I get it now. I mean, for some bizarre reason, not everyone has emotional breakdowns in the middle of watching David Attenborough's, *Our Planet*...but I actually feel like they should!

All my life I've been told -as I bet you have too- to "tone it down" and "play it cool." First off, I'm totally cool, dude, why don't *you* tone it down? And secondly, since when is it a crime or a bad thing to feel everything super-intensely?

Shouldn't the people who DON'T feel this way be the ones begging to experience what we do?

I mean, sure, would I rather not feel like my whole body is breaking when a character I love dies on TV? Yeah, I guess a part of me would be relieved. But also, like, what even is the point in living if you're not going to be able to really *feel* something?

Didn't the people who made the TV shows intend on having us experience an emotional reaction of some kind? They probably didn't expect full-on breakdowns, but hey, they should be flattered! They say imitation is the sincerest form of flattery - well I think having someone go through an emotional break from your work is the actual sincerest form of flattery.

Maybe you're like this too? The kid who cried so hard during that scene where they had to put Old Yeller down that they called home* because they didn't know what to do with you? (*this story is not mine, but a friend of mine, unfortunately my teachers just let me cry and didn't send me home for it) Or that time you watched Titanic when you were only ten years old* and could barely talk to people for three weeks? (*this one is 100% what happened to me) Perhaps you were the first kid in a teacher's 20 years of teaching to protest collecting insects* because it was cruel. (*she ended up having me collect already dead ones...and it still broke my heart)

People don't know how to handle us. They try to shape and conform us to fit into their mold because it's more comfortable for *them*.

It's OKAY to be intense. It is not a weakness, it is a strength!

Now, are there times it feels totally overwhelming and uncool?

Yep!

But, just like any superhero who first discovers their powers, we have to learn how to use them.

Think about what happened when Spider-Man first got bit by a radio-active spider. Did he know how to be a hero right away? Uh, not in the slightest. He could have said, "screw this, this is too much for me" and done his best to suppress his spidey-sense and super agility, but no, he rose to the occasion and even enhanced his power with his own creation of special webbing.

I'm not gonna ask you to go out and create your own citizen-protecting webbing, but as we go on you will create your own metaphorical webbing, *for sure.*

△△△

You ever watch a superhero movie or read a comic book and think, "I could never be that brave! How do they do it?"

Darling, simply by being an intense human, you *are* that brave.

You have a great power, and with it, a great responsibility.

Think of this book as your training to use your powers for justice.

CHAPTER 3: PREPARE YOURSELF

HAVING A POWER ISN'T WHAT MAKES YOU A HERO - IT'S HOW YOU USE IT THAT DOES.

Plenty of people with our level of intensity do not choose to put in the work you're about to put in to use their power for good. Being intense in and of itself is not the power, *but what you do with it is*.

I want to start by saying how excited I am that you are making this commitment - and I hope you are too. This isn't for people just dabbling in learning how to work with their intensity. No, this is the real deal, let's-be-heroes-for-the-rest-of-our-lives kind of work we are going to do.

I want to prepare you that doing this *is work.* It may be the best work you will ever do, but it's a daily commitment.

All of the lessons in this book come from my experience journeying to stable, maintainable harmony with my emotions from deep, dark depression, mania, and anxiety (and at times all in one day due to rapid-cycling).

I was told by nearly a dozen mental health professionals that I would have to be medicated for the rest of my life.

I was told my mental illnesses would run the show unless I was, to some degree, sedated.

I have spent the past six years doing the work I will teach you in this book, and now I have over three years of using my emotions as my strength, without the assistance of medications. As mentioned, this work can be done with or without medications - it really isn't even about that, it's just that in a world where we're often told we're "*too much*" it's important to know that isn't necessarily true.

Your sensitivities can be your strength if used properly.

I have to make a choice *every single day* to keep doing the work I teach in this book. Sometimes it's painful. Sometimes it's grueling. Sometimes it's really messy and uncomfortable. That's part of being a superhero.

And, the good news is, this work allows us to use our intense emotions for good, instead of feeling like they're working against us.

Once you work *with* them, instead of being at the mercy *of* them, they become an amazing source of guidance and inspiration.

In order to be successful in this practice, we must prepare ourselves.

Imagine you've just been brought to a giant courtroom full of all your most respected heroes. You could see these as fictional heroes or real life idols. See yourself stepping up to the judge and declaring the following message to the room. If you're in a private space right now, say it out-loud. If you're reading this on a train, maybe just think it in your head:

"I am ready for this new chapter of my life. I am done being victim to the ups and downs of my intense emotionality. I am ready to rise. Like a phoenix from the ashes, I am ready to become the fully embodied best version of myself, complete with the positive uses of my superpower. I am ready, and I promise to myself and everyone in this room that I will rise."

Take a deep breath in through your nose and out through your mouth.

Feel the power of this statement. Feel the power of

all those who've walked before you - all the heroes you look up to, real and imagined - holding space for you to make this commitment.

To deepen this, if you can, take a moment now to write yourself a letter declaring your intent to commit to this work in your own words.

I recommend preparing your space by lighting a candle, putting on some music, really making it a special experience; a celebration. Maybe even having a piece of chocolate to eat afterwards.

This commitment you are making can be a major turning point in your life, *or* you can not take it seriously and it can just be another day where things stay the same. The choice is yours. Neither one is right or wrong.

If you've decided to make this commitment, you deserve to feel pride and respect towards yourself for making it. If you focus on feeling proud of yourself for this commitment, you will naturally attract more feelings of self-pride - which is a gateway to increased self-love and self-worth, both of which are key components to embracing your inner hero that we will grow on our journey together.

For right now, I'm hoping you're feeling good about making a commitment to yourself, but even if you're actually just feeling scared, uncertain, or doubtful, that's cool too. Honor it. Accept it. Feel it. It's okay to feel whatever you feel.

"I'm accepting my emotions. Yay!"

Say this to yourself *anytime* you let yourself accept an emotion from this point forward. **Good, bad, doesn't matter.** Point it out to yourself. Celebrate yourself for the fact that you are accepting how you feel.

A big part of the struggle that comes with being sensitive is that we receive the message at a very early age that feeling sad, or down, or angry (or any other "undesirable" emotion) is a very bad thing.

It's not bad!

Because we're told it's bad, we then feel shame when we feel down, and beat ourselves up for it, all the while trying to hide it and act like we feel okay. This in turn only makes us feel worse.

What would happen if we were told that all of our emotions are valid and useful and we should never feel ashamed for anything we feel?

Accepting yourself for feeling however you feel, is one of the deepest acts of self love possible. Even if you currently feel like there's very little self-love going down in your life, that's okay. Accept that that's what's happening and instantly a tiny little shift will occur because you accepted that emotion - yay!

I'm going to give you a checklist to help you prepare for having the most success working with this book.

That said, even if you are someone who just randomly picks up books and reads sporadically (my hand is up), trust you'll get whatever content you need.

Here's my recommended checklist to get started:

☒ Declare a statement of commitment (YAY! You already did this!)

❏ Sign up for my year of free weekly meditations. They're designed to be a perfect companion for this book. You can find them at www.marisaimon.com/freemeditations

❏ Set aside at least five minutes/day for meditation and self-care. While I suggest a minimum of five minutes, know that the more you put in, the more you get out. Do what you can. In Chapter 17 I give you ideas and practices for what to do with this time.

❏ Get yourself a beautiful journal that excites you to use. Always have your journal handy while you're reading this book because I will assign random journaling exercises throughout this process.

❏ Make sleep a priority. More on this in Chapter 16.

❏ Prepare yourself mentally by reminding yourself everyday that this is a process. Read the "IMPORTANT REMINDER" below. Perhaps type or write a copy and keep it somewhere you'll often see it.

Super Intense

Heartfelt Double-Check: Did you get your year of free superhero meditations yet? No strings attached, but it isn't for everyone. It's a commitment. Every Monday for a year you'll get a meditation and an exercise designed to help you feel like you are your own superhero. Go to marisaimon.com/free-meditations to learn more. And if you'd like to find out what your hero name is, go to marisaimon.com/heroquiz!

IMPORTANT REMINDER:

You are *practicing* at living in harmony with your emotions to use your sensitivity for good. Everything we learn takes time and patience and most importantly, practice. No matter how much time you spend staring at music notes in your "How to Learn Piano" book, it won't help you play piano until you actually sit down and practice.

DO NOT be bumming about not instantly feeling like your life is changing or that it isn't coming easily. While you might experience positive change overnight, it very well may take a long commitment of practice. How many people do you know who can sit down at a piano and play Mozart's *Moonlight Sonata* without ever having been taught how?

We all have to learn every single skill we have. Many of us were never *taught* how to accept our emotions and work with our sensitivities. In fact, we were taught the opposite. So this process might take time.

So what?

Timing always works out perfectly. Just stay faithful to yourself and all the love that is around you - whether you feel like you're surrounded by love or not.

Also, be proud of yourself. Celebrate every small win. Every time you lovingly accept your emotions (the good and the bad) is equivalent to every time you learn a new song. Maybe you start working with your feelings in a way that's similar to playing *Mary Had a Little Lamb*, but then you move up to a way that's like learning how to play *Rhapsody in Blue*! **Each new level of working with feelings is a win.**

Children have piano recitals to show off even the most boring songs because they're proud that they learned it! I think the ability to celebrate even the tiniest of wins is a wonderful skill to cultivate.

CHAPTER 4: IT STARTS...

I don't remember a lot from my sophomore semester in college when I experienced my first manic episode. That moment where I was overlooking the swan pond, I knew for sure that I was a superhero here to fight all injustices in this world.

Unfortunately, on any given moment I also believed I was an evil villain sent to destroy the superhero version of myself. As soon as the hero would get to work, the villain would do whatever she could stop her. You can imagine how messy this became.

At this point in my life leading up to this, I hadn't yet been diagnosed with bipolar disorder. In fact, I had only *just* been diagnosed a few months earlier with depression, anxiety, ADD, insomnia and bulimia - even though the earliest I can remember feeling long-lasting, life-impacting depression was age ten, and I started binging and purging at fifteen to

Super Intense

cope with anxiety. I never could focus in class and got by because I had friends who always made sure I knew what class to go to when and what homework was due (heaven forbid I kept track of my own schedule...also, awesome friends, right?). And I never would have considered myself someone who *sleeps* - even as an infant (sorry for all that night time screaming mom and dad!).

Looking back now and recognizing how I experienced extended periods of intense lows and highs all my life, coupled with difficulty sleeping, it all feels so obvious. But at the time I thought bipolar just meant someone who was "moody" - something I thought was totally lame, because I proudly was way more intense than just being moody. I had no idea it was a serious condition that could result in clinical insanity.

And then, there I was...

Convinced my friends were plotting against me any time I wasn't around...

(Who "plots" against people anyway?)

Watching my face shape shift in the mirror every night after my roommates went to bed...

Listening to aliens talk to me through my headphones that weren't plugged into anything...

And of course...spending time as a hero here to save the world, *or* an evil villain trying to destroy the hero version of me.

Finally a dear friend called my parents and so began the process of getting professional help.

I withdrew from school, was released into my parents custody, and given a blend of several medications (they called it a cocktail, how fun?) that left me in a stupor. I was dazed in a lay-z-boy in their house for weeks.

At first I didn't want to be drugged. I had fallen in love with the euphoric feeling of being a superhero - how on Earth could I go back to being a *commoner?*

Ugh.

But, I let them medicate me, all the while thinking secretly, "someday I'll pretend I'm on meds and I won't be and they won't even know - then I can return to my greatness."

I thought my greatness lived within the super-intense high of mania.

I've learned that it lives within me only in a state of balance.

I did eventually pretend to be on meds while being off of them and it was the *stupidest*, least safe thing ever and it failed many times. I do **not** recommend it.

But, eventually mania lost its allure when I started finding stable inner peace and happiness - this is a feeling I would never again trade for the unstable euphoria…

Especially now that I know the truth.

While the doctors may refer to my belief that I was a superhero as a "delusion," now I understand that I was right about it all along.

But now, that inner villain trying to destroy the hero version of myself is just the side of me that experiences fear and anxiety. There's nothing wrong with that side of me. I welcome it with love and let it express itself safely now. It's like when Bruce Banner works in harmony with Hulk.

Not everyone can feel things intensely, my friend. I think of us as a breed not that dissimilar to mutants in the Marvel Universe - humans who have special abilities that the world doesn't understand. Society thinks their mutations are an unsafe problem for the world. While, yes, some mutants end up using their abilities for crime and general evil-doings, many use their powers for good. We just need to learn how to be like the X-Men who use their special abilities for good so that society can start to recognize that there is nothing wrong with being super-intense.

Actually, scrap that, we don't want them just to feel like there's nothing wrong with it - we want them to see the *value* in it! It's crazy valuable, man (or woman, or human, whatever you prefer me to call you).

I promise you.

CHAPTER 5: VIRTUAL REALITY

"You think you know how the world works? You think that this material universe is all there is? What is real? What mysteries lie beyond the reach of your senses? At the root of existence, mind and matter meet. Thoughts form reality...who are you in this vast multiverse, Mr. Strange?"

~The Ancient One, From Doctor Strange

The first lesson in your hero training is about how important it is to understand the power of your mind.

You create your own reality. I don't need to get super deep in quantum mechanics, I'm sure you're well versed in string theory any way (who isn't, amiright?), but long story short and definitely not scientific: reality is basically whatever you choose it to be.

Without our thoughts, which create our beliefs - what are we? Who are we?

Regardless of whether or not science actually proves that our thoughts create our reality, you don't have to be a genius (which quite frankly I'm sure you are, if you're reading this) to know that when you choose to see the world as cruel and unfair, it appears cruel and unfair - when you choose to see love and goodness, all of a sudden you can't help but notice love and goodness.

Try this experiment: How often do you think you see hair scrunchies? Feels like an outdated style that I literally never see. Not that I'm knocking it, I'm actually quite a fan - but it's not super popular right now. So the experiment is to count how many you see in the course of the next seven days. You'll start to feel like they're *everywhere*, on *everyone.* You'll see them on people you pass on the street, on characters in shows you watch (if you watch Seinfeld regularly you could probably make a game out of it), and you'll even start noticing them more in stores and maybe even advertisements.

Our observations totally affect our reality, but really, our *beliefs* about those observations come first. I believe I never see scrunchies, so I don't. *(Fun side note: it's now been a week since I wrote this chapter and I'm starting to see them everywhere, on everyone)*

If our beliefs affect how we observe and interact

with the world, who creates our beliefs?

Are we born with them?

Now that's a deep question that I don't have the answer to, but I do know that not that long ago I believed I was an unworthy, unlovable person, who would never find success or happiness doing something I love. It wasn't true, ever, but it was *true to me* because I believed it, and so I saw it in the world around me. And thus, it became my truth.

If it's hard to identify in yourself right now, it might be easier to spot what I'm talking about by considering someone close to you who keeps making - what you feel - are the same mistakes in their life. Maybe they keep ending up in jobs that make them feel miserable, or relationships where their partner takes them for granted. You can see clearly as an outside observer that it doesn't have to be this way. But to them, it might feel like there is no other way so they keep ending up in situations that prove their worldview...no matter how much you advise them against it.

I spent six years working to change the belief that I was unworthy. My friends already knew it wasn't true. All my life they'd try to cheer me up. Tell me how great I am. That I should be happy.

One night I locked myself in a closet at a sleepover party in high school, sobbing about what a horrible person I was - I was the only one who could see it. No one else knew it to be true, so it wasn't true to them. I believed it was my truth, so *to me*, it was.

The last time you were depressed (maybe it's right now), did you have people telling you that you should be happy? Isn't it the worst?

You know their intentions are good. You know they mean well. You know you probably *should* be happy.

So why is it so annoying to be told that?

It's because it goes directly against a belief you are holding within you. A belief that you are depressed. A belief that it's too hard to change. A belief that it's hopeless.

It annoys you for the same reason you feel like scratching someone's eyeballs out when you play them your favorite song - you know the one that gives you goosebumps all over? - and they go, "I don't really like that song."

How could they not like the best song ever? What is wrong with them???

It's the same annoying feeling we have when we wonder, how could they tell us to be happy when we clearly can't be?

We get frustrated because it goes against what we feel and what we believe. And depression is one of the hardest beliefs to change, in my experience.

But when we start accepting that we are the ones

who choose our beliefs, and that everyone else is choosing their own, we can't take it personally any more. Their thoughts and opinions have nothing to do with us and everything to do with their own beliefs and biases.

Once I realized I can create my own reality by changing my beliefs, I started to get curious about where my beliefs came from anyway.

Like, why did I believe I couldn't call myself a musician even though I had been writing music for over two decades? Why did I feel it necessary to cross the street if I was going to be approaching a man on the same sidewalk I was on?

Beliefs don't appear for no reason. If we're not choosing them for ourselves, then society and outside influences are choosing them for us.

Yuck.

Wouldn't you rather be in control of what you believe? I have to check my thoughts all the time to try to make sure it's my own belief, opinion or thought and not something I was influenced to feel. I think it's harder than ever right now because of social media.

It's not too dissimilar to when a child says something that was clearly just a regurgitation of what they heard an adult say. I was once babysitting a six year old who noticed a man in a business suit, and the kid said "Ew! A business suit! Gross, I'd never want to be a businessman wearing a suit, they are so full of themselves!" First I was like, this kid's *so* cool. Then I was like, also wait, why does he even know the phrase *business suit*? It's not like he's shopping for them!

Although that'd be pretty cool too.

He must have heard an adult say how "full of themselves" businessmen are.

We do the same thing all the time. We hear an opinion somewhere and we take it on as our own. But it's often way sneakier than that. Years of seeing men play superheroes in movies growing up led many women to think they can only be the damsel in distress and not the hero. Fortunately with role models like Wonder Woman and Captain Marvel, young humans are being raised with much different stories.

So if ideas and opinions may be ingrained from subconscious programming, how do we know if it's something we truly believe on a deeper level?

The answer is easy, but in practice it's a good amount of work: We have to get really intimate with ourselves. We have to spend time in quiet meditation, just with ourselves, uninterrupted by outside influence and truly *listen*. We have a deep inner wisdom within us that once tapped into can lead to a pretty easy and blissed out way to live in connection with your own truth.

Once we do this, we can get really clear on what we *want* to believe.

This is why I *want* you to be discerning with what I'm saying. If you don't agree, great! If you do, great! Just allow yourself to find *your own* reality. It may not be the same as mine and I give you tools throughout the book - **especially Chapter 10** - to help you gain more clarity around this.

For now the most important thing is to just be open and aware of the fact that the things you may believe may not be true - and it's **time to choose what you'd like to have as your reality instead of letting years of programming from society, friends and family choose it for you.**

△△△

If you're reading this right now and you're in the middle of depression, first off, congrats! I never found it easy to read when I was depressed - especially not something that would be helpful. You freaking rock!!!

Secondly, it can feel a lot harder to change your thoughts when you're clinically depressed but there is a way around it. And as you'll learn, there's nothing wrong with feeling the way you feel. Chapter 10 gets much deeper in how this works. Hang in there.

CHAPTER 6: BAD

A note on things we refer to as "bad."

When I was a kid my parents would always give me this super awesome parable that somehow eventually sank into my subconsciousness and helped shaped the way I work with my emotions.

I didn't know it at the time, but this story I thought was flat-out boring as a kid was actually changing the course of my life. Good job, mom and dad!

Here's my version of the story I was told. Believe it or not, this is watered down compared to how they would've told it.

Okay, here it goes:

Back in old-timey days, I assume somewhere in Europe, there once was a farmer who's newly 18-year-old son had an accident that caused him to break his leg.

Everyone in the town felt so bad for this farmer, for they knew he needed help around the farm and now that his son could not help him, he may have a less profitable season.

They all pitied the farmer. Every time the farmer would bump into someone in town they'd stop him and say "We're so sorry for you. What bad luck you have."

The farmer was never phased or worried about it. He'd say: "Good luck, bad luck, who's to say?"

Shortly after, a war broke out and every 18-year-old male was drafted to fight. When the soldiers came for the farmers son, he was exempt from having to fight because of his broken leg. While many others in the community lost their sons in war, the farmer's was safe at home.

Good luck, bad luck, who's to say?

The story actually continues to more scenarios. At one point their only horse runs away and everyone pities the guy again, but the next year the horse returns with an entire family of horses which triples the farmer's business.

Essentially what became part of my understanding is that we don't actually know if something is good or bad in any given moment, but we're constantly assigning the title of "bad" to everything that remotely appears that way. And in fact we're often much, much quicker at assigning something as bad, than we are at assigning something as good.

If we take that title away and accept things as they are, we can remove a lot of the discomfort of many situations. We don't have the full scope of what's happening in the greater scheme of things. Why stress ourselves out over calling something bad? Especially when we are the ones responsible for our own perspective!

Why this is so important in your superhero training is that I want you to stop yourself every time you label an emotion as bad and instead you can ask yourself, "good, bad, who's to say?"

It will make the rest of this work so much easier if you get on board with the fact that no emotion is bad unless you choose to see it that way.

CHAPTER 7: TAKE RESPONSIBILITY

Not that long ago, I thought I was a complete victim to my emotions. I believed the way I felt was 100% the fault of the outside world and genetics.

I believed there was no other way, nor any other explanation for why I felt the way I did.

Today I take responsibility.

And to be a hero, you must too.

Sorry, sugar, if it's a tough pill to swallow but I told you it wouldn't always be easy.

And also, sorry I called you sugar. I don't think I've ever called anyone sugar before.

That said, it doesn't have to be as hard as you'd think either.

When you accept how you feel with love, instead of judging yourself for however you feel, you're automatically taking the first step in owning your responsibility.

See? You're already halfway there, isn't that so much easier?

Right now if you're like, "but my boss is a jerk and is ruining my life," I hear you - the outside world does stuff. But we control the inside world: our hearts, our minds.

We can't control everything that's happening all around us, but we can control how we respond (although in Chapter 11 I'll explain something that will challenge this just a little bit, and it's awesome, hang tight).

It takes practice - just like any new skill. So don't beat yourself up even if several years from now you still find yourself blaming everyone around you for your misery. As long as you take steps daily, over time you'll notice a positive difference.

Just like any hero, we are often given challenges with recurring themes. For most superheroes a common theme is helping others at the risk of losing the ones they love, either literally or just through strained relationships. I actually don't believe us real life heroes have to go through that specific situation, but we have our own recurring situations for sure. For me, the recurring challenge I was faced with was speaking up for myself.

I kept being placed in different scenarios where I was given an opposer of some kind who would yell at me, belittle me, and take advantage of me.

Often the person creating this conflict would be someone I could not avoid - like a boss, a coworker, a close friend or a romantic partner.

Just like in a video game, it was like each new scenario was a new level and I could not move on to the next one until I successfully completed the first.

I spent about five years climbing the different levels of this challenge. When I first owned my responsibility in it, I realized that just because someone's veins are popping out as they yell at me over what they perceive to be *my* problems, doesn't mean I need to feel as horrible as *they* do.

I have every right to feel good. And so do you. We all do. Just because someone else does something that is potentially threatening to our happiness and wellbeing, doesn't mean they have complete control over it. How someone else feels about us, has nothing to do with us. We are not responsible for anyone else's actions or happiness - only our own. That's why we must take this responsibility seriously.

Here are the 5 steps I take and recommend to make this process easier:

1. See the outside world as separate

You can use a visualization of an orb of light or a column of light separating you from everything around you. You can also visualize borders of flowers, or rainbows or anything else that feels good to you. The more fun you have with it, the better it works, and the easier it is to do. I get pretty Lisa Frank-y sometimes with the visualizations I choose.

In the scenario I shared earlier, (where someone's veins were literally popping out of their face and neck as they screamed at me), before I started using this visualization process, I would shake uncontrollably when being in that situation. I would then leave the room and cry.

When I started seeing that this person is separate from me, and having their own experience, I realized that I didn't have to take on their feelings as my own. I imagined us both in columns of blue light with red roses between us and I enjoy the peaceful world I created for myself. The world I deserved.

While this person's actions did not change, *I* changed how I felt about them. I no longer found myself shaking uncontrollably or having to leave and cry. I found my center and knew that that person's lack of ability to control their emotions was on them, *not* on me.

2. See everyone as the small child version of themselves.

Just because we all grow into bigger bodies, doesn't mean everyone is a well-adjusted adult. A lot of people are carrying around wounds from childhood and taking those wounds out on the world around them. Viewing them as a small (and often scared) child allows you to have more compassion and not take things as personally. This is especially true of our parents.

We tend to hold people we look up to, like parents, supervisors and mentors, to higher standards. We often think they must be better than us in some way. But really, they're just figuring out life like the rest of us. We're all just figuring it out. We all have wounds. We all have scars. We're all hurting on the inside in some way.

When you see someone as a child - especially as a small, scared child - it's so much easier to let them off the hook and to not take their acting out personally. There's a bit more on this in Chapter 13.

3. Be clear on how you want to feel.

If you aren't clear on how you want to feel you'll be put in all sorts of "training arenas" designed to help you gain that clarity - but you might not be happy with how you have to gain it.

I didn't realize I wanted to be respected and treated with respect. You might think that should be an obvious thing, but for some reason it just wasn't obvious to me. I was put in scenario after scenario where I had to learn more and more about how I desired to be treated. Once I got clear on it, everything became easier and I was faced with fewer and fewer settings that challenged that desire within me.

4. Make the choice daily to observe your reactions.

As you observe how you react to things you can see if you're giving your power to someone else or if you're taking it in your own hands.

For example, when I was at a job where the supervisor would berate me for something beyond my control, I used to give this person more power by letting it hurt me. I had to observe this and be aware of it in order to make a change.

When I instead chose to take steps number 1 and 2 and take action from my own sense of identity and strength, my reactions were calm. They gave *me* more power because they came from a place of love and acceptance towards myself instead of fear and reactivity to another person. You'll only be able to consciously choose how you react when you start observing yourself.

5. Appreciate yourself during this process.

Every time you choose to take responsibility, don't just shrug it off like it's no big deal. You're growing a new muscle. Be proud of it. Be grateful. Take time to appreciate yourself for the little changes. The more you appreciate yourself the easier this work will be.

Actually, take a moment right now to take a deep breath and feel appreciation towards yourself for the work you've done so far - no matter how big or small. At the top of the breath, hold it in and let the feelings of appreciation build. When you're ready, exhale with a long audible sigh.

CHAPTER 8: FEELINGS SPEAK LOUDER THAN WORDS

Positive affirmations are statements about yourself and your life that are designed to produce a positive outcome in emotion.

As mentioned, how we feel affects the world around us. This is why shifting how we feel can powerfully shift everything else as well.

However, this is also why no amount of positive affirmations can create the change you're seeking. Probably sounds contradictory but it's not.

Hear me out.

If you're going through intense anxiety and you affirm: "I'm relaxed," do you *actually* feel relaxed?

If that works for you - awesome!

If it doesn't, then you are like most people. In this case it's important to come up with affirmations that help you shift forward. You can't just affirm something that *feels like a lie to you* and then have a shift in emotion. Affirmations are powerful, but only when we choose ones that feel true or possible to us.

The reason we're discussing this now is that in Chapter 10, you will learn what I believe to be one of the most important exercises in the book. As part of this exercise, you will be working on changing beliefs. This is much like writing your own affirmations. If you write an affirmation that you cannot believe in, then your feelings around it will not change.

You gotta believe in the affirmation you are writing or saying because really, *it's just words.* What makes it real is how you feel.

Ooh! That's a fun rhyme:

"What makes it real is how you feel."

That goes for pretty much everything.

It's not what you say that matters, but how you feel about what you say. If you want to feel peaceful but saying "I feel peaceful" just makes you feel resentful that you don't feel peaceful, well then you're just perpetuating the belief that you're not peaceful.

If you want to feel peaceful but aren't sure if you can feel that way so you say "I am willing to believe I can feel peaceful," now you step into the energy of willingness. If you're *willing* to have a new belief, anything is possible!

I just want you to be aware of this because your body always knows how you feel. You can't trick it. You can't just slap a sticker on it and *pretend* to feel differently than you do. It's not fair to your emotions anyway.

Chapter 10 is all about learning how to shift the feelings, but I want to share this first because I don't want you faking any part of this process. If you're trying to come up with new positive beliefs, it's important to choose wording like "I am *willing* to believe," or "I think it's possible to believe," or "I am ready for a change" - versus language that doesn't feel true to you.

Ready hero? We'll dive in soon, but first, one more important note in Chapter 9…

CHAPTER 9: BREAKDOWN

The next chapter is my favorite tool in working with your emotional intensity (I use it daily), but I want to tell you this first and here's why: Just because I'm teaching you how to move through your feelings doesn't mean not to let them express themselves first if they need to.

If you're gonna breakdown, breakdown.

Don't hold it in just to act strong. It's *stronger* to *feel* your emotions.

Find a private, safe space and let it all out. Put on some screamo, country, trap, whatever gets you moving and let your feelings express themselves.

Not every feeling needs it's own show, but you'll know the ones that do. When you truly feel like you can't hold it in and might break at any moment is a beautiful time to break.

Scream into a pillow.

Stomp on the floor.

Dance like a weirdo.

Sob.

It's all good man, get it out. Don't judge yourself, just give yourself the gift of moving it through you by letting it express itself in whatever safe and private way you enjoy.

I personally just like to cry really loudly. It feels horrible and great at the same time.

Sometimes I cry loudly while dancing/stomping around to music. It's one of the least attractive things anyone could do, but you know what's less attractive? Acting like you're okay your whole life when everyone can tell that you're not. Don't do that to people. Take time for yourself to express your emotions. There's nothing wrong with them and in the next chapter you'll see how useful they really are!

CHAPTER 10: FEAR IS FOR CHAMPIONS

"YOU ARE STRONGER THAN YOU BELIEVE. YOU HAVE GREATER POWERS THAN YOU KNOW."

~Antiope
From Wonder Woman

Have you ever heard the phrases, "fear isn't real" or "fear is a liar"?

First of all, since we create our reality with our thoughts, if we feel fear - then it's real *to us* as long as we're feeling it.

Secondly, even if it is a liar, it doesn't mean it's useless. Doesn't mean it should be ignored or pushed past.

No emotion we experience is without its purpose.

Everything we feel is for a reason and fear is no different. We can't shun it. In fact, in my experience, every single time I ever tried to run away from fear and act like it didn't exist, it just grew louder in the background until I was forced to recognize it.

Maybe this happened to you too - you worked a job that you hated but were too scared to do anything about it until the job got so intolerable you had no other choice? Same thing can happen in relationships, our home life, our health, and any other aspect of our lives when we ignore the fear until it forces us to pay attention.

Since that's going to happen anyway, uh....forgive me for stating the obvious here, but....why are we not facing it before it forces us to?

Seems silly to have to even ask or suggest, but I know full well what it's like to pretend fear doesn't exist and act like it's not real.

It's okay to feel fear and I truly believe that to live the life we want, it all starts with embracing fear. Fear is just a wounded part of you wishing you'd turn around and give it a big hug.

The good news is, since you're reading this book, you're probably riddled with fear. This might not feel like good news right now, but it totally is and you'll soon see why.

In case you're like, "I'm not riddled with fear, I'm

the bravest person in the world!" I just want to note: Fear doesn't always manifest as being something obvious. If you ever feel anxiety, hesitancy, depression, loneliness, failure, discouragement, or any other emotion you don't particularly love - you better believe what lies beneath that feeling is fear.

And there's absolutely nothing wrong with it.

Fear is for champions, and that's what you are. The more fear you have, the more passionate of a person you are and the more opportunities you have to follow your passions.

It's simple logic. If you fear anything, it's because you strongly desire its opposite.

For example - if you fear being eaten by monsters when the lights go out (not that I *totally* feel that way - I'm more nervous about something reaching up from under my bed and grabbing my arm if I let it hang over the side, if I'm being perfectly honest) - anyway, if you're afraid of being eaten, it must mean you have a strong desire to have your body in full functioning form; healthy and free.

Okay, let's use this on something more realistic. Say you're feeling very lonely. Beneath that feeling of loneliness is a fear of being alone, right? That fear indicates a strong desire to feel loved.

People who don't experience intense negative emotions are usually not as passionate about their desires.

They don't feel as lonely because they don't care as much about feeling loved. They don't get as discouraged because they don't care as much about their dreams. They don't get as heartbroken because they never loved as strongly as you did.

Experiencing a lot of fear-based emotions indicates that you are an incredibly passionate human being.

The worse you feel, the stronger you want the opposite of whatever fear is beneath your emotion. You are passionate, this is why you get so down so easily! (And why you get emotionally high so easily).

This is why fears are awesome and why you are awesome for having them. Living in harmony with my fears is truly the lion's share of the work involved in using my intensity for heroic good.

It all starts by letting yourself actually witness and observe your fears.

Fears are like the rumble strips - the little bumpy parts on the side of the road designed to wake you up if you fall asleep while driving. They're guide posts. Again: They're useful. And they are *not* bad.

When I first started working with my fears it was actually hard to identify them right away. They were *so* ingrained in every aspect of my day I didn't exactly notice it.

In meetings when I would hesitate to say something: that was fear.

At home when I'd overthink what to text my crush of the moment: that was fear.

In the mornings when I'd try on several outfits and hate how every single one looked on me: fear.

It seems obvious now, but those tiny moments were so common in my day it took legitimate analyzing to recognize them. This is because we're deeply accustomed to running away from fears and acting like they don't exist. We often don't notice them until they're crippling us with anxiety, depression or despair of some kind.

The important thing about changing our awareness around this is that we're not doing it to beat ourselves up for being so fearful. We're not doing it to feel shame over feeling fear. **We're doing it to recognize how amazing we are.**

Every time you have the tiniest of fears, it's just giving you guidance. You are amazing for experiencing fear-based feelings because it shows how well guided you are.

Welcome in your fears because they are not your enemy. The enemy is the thought that they are bad

Super Intense

and something to ignore.

Just so you know, I'm writing this chapter *as* I feel horrible. And I'm not yet 100% sure why.

My heart is pounding. My chest feels tight. I feel simultaneously like falling asleep, eating an entire tub of peanut butter, and crying.

I'm not gonna say it doesn't suck to feel horrible.

But I'm also not going to run away from it.

I recently heard an interview on *Girlboss Radio* with Valerie Jarrett, a former senior advisor to Barack Obama, about his leadership style that actually is the perfect metaphor for my goal with handling my emotions.

She said that President Obama was always seeking out ways to get the opinions of everyone in a room during meetings. If someone was quiet or too scared to speak up, he'd talk to them privately and encourage them to share their opinion. If someone disagreed with him, he wanted to know.

According to the interview, he welcomed all messages equally and sought out all sides. Not with judgement, but with openness and curiosity.

The way he managed his staff is how *we* need to play the role of manager with our emotions.

We need to be like Obama when it comes to those quiet voices in our heads (or sometimes those loud unruly ones) that make us uncomfortable to lean into. Imagine yourself as the cool, unflappable leader just giving that emotion its chance to speak up. Let yourself be the one to listen, to learn, to be curious while the emotion shares whatever it has to share.

When we give it a space to speak up, we lessen the impact. Have you ever met someone who avoids speaking up at all costs until they can't hold it in any longer and they just blow up? Your emotions will do the same thing.

Another way to look at it is as if you are the conductor of an orchestra and each instrument is a different emotion. Yes an emotion like shame might have solos sometimes, but *you* are the one choosing when it plays, how long, and how loud.

Will you just ignore the emotion and act like it doesn't exist? Or will you lean in and get curious? Will you listen?

Here's the process:

I talk to the emotion. I name it whatever it feels like, let's say in this instance, "failure," and then I go:

Hi failure, what's up?

And I listen. Right now, here's what failure is saying:

"Who are you to try to help anyone use their emotions as a superpower when you are such a failure at it yourself? Look at how you feel right now!"

I imagine myself like Obama, cool-headed, easy-going, super attractive, and open to listening to the emotion.

> Furthermore, I treat it like a small child. Like it is worthy of love and respect. I listen with my heart. I welcome in what it has to say.

I then get clear on what it wants to teach me. If I'm afraid of being a failure at helping people use their emotional intensity as a superpower - then it must mean it is very important to me. It must mean I deeply *desire* for these words to inspire, encourage, motivate and support.

That's awesome! That fear-based emotion just gave me fabulous, beautiful insight. As soon as I recognize it, I can feel myself shifting out of the fear of failure and into the excitement of helping others.

After I hear it out, I imagine myself taking it by the hand and thanking it for being brave enough to tell me how it feels.

"Thank you failure! Thank you for showing up."

I mean what harm can it do to welcome it in - it's a feeling within you! <u>It's already there anyway</u> - it cannot possibly do any more harm to welcome it in with wide open loving arms, than it does to shun it.

Finally I welcome in a new belief. Since I'm the one

responsible for creating my own beliefs, once I recognize one that isn't serving me, I can use it to guide me towards one that does. This shifts how I'm feeling even more.

I will give you a chart you can use as a journal exercise to do this process daily, but for now I want to explain further what's going on here and why this very simple process works.

Essentially what is happening is I am guiding myself through the emotional scale.

Like we discussed in Chapter 8 - it's very difficult to move out of depression into a state of happiness. That's because it's a long journey from here to there.

However, if we move just one emotion at a time - much like moving through squares on a board game - we can eventually get there.

Take a look at the following diagram.

In this chart you see various categories of emotions, spanning from total despair to pure joy.

While you may not be able to flick a switch and move from total despair to joy, you can move from total despair to unworthiness, right? They're really not that far away from each other. If you know what one feels like, you likely know what the other does. From unworthiness you can likely move into blaming others and perhaps getting angry. From anger you can move into just being frustrated. Frustration can lead to a state of being neutral - not happy, not sad, just existing. Neutrality can lead to contentment. Contentment can lead to optimism, which leads to enthusiasm and finally - pure joy!

It's like a road map!

Pure Joy
In this state you feel blissful, empowered and like life is easy.

Enthusiasm
In this state you experience deep appreciation and excitement for life.

Optimism
In this category you feel hopeful and positive.

Contentment
In this state, you feel okay. You may not be super happy, but you feel pretty good.

Neutral
This is a state of feeling "empty" - can be beautiful when it's caused by mindfulness, can be potentially challenging when it's out of numbness.

Frustration
In this state you may be doubtful, uncertain and fed up.

Anger
This moves up one step from the previous emotion where you move away from attacking yourself, to attacking others. You may feel jealousy or rage.

Self-Attack
In this state you blame and shame yourself. You feel unworthy and experience a lot of self-inflicted guilt.

Total Despair
This is the state where everything feels hopeless/useless/pointless, and you experience intense self-loathing and depression.

I've seen charts like this in various places. My favorite resource, if you'd like to dig a lot deeper into this, is Melody Fletcher's book: "*Deliberate Receiving:*

Finally, the Universe Makes Some Freakin' Sense!"

But you don't have to go much deeper to see how empowering and helpful a map like this is.

This is why if I tap into feelings of failure that live somewhere around self-attack, I can move up into optimism and eventually enthusiasm - all by simply looking at my fears and anxieties with love.

When we instead just try to ignore them, we are not offering ourselves any way up and out.

Fears are great because they help guide us towards our deepest desires and enthusiasm for life when we work <u>with</u> them, instead of running <u>away from</u> them.

Here's your assignment:

At the end of each day - or at whatever time works for you - fill in the following grid. Follow each step in order. You can just write it as steps in your journal.

Before you start, take a moment to get centered. Let yourself sit in a quiet place and take three deep breaths. Welcome in the super-hero version of yourself. Be open, willing and ready to welcome in your emotions with love.

No emotion is bad, and there is never a need to judge

yourself or sugarcoat how you feel. State it as it is, and know that that's okay.

Essentially this process moves you from any feeling you have that's below neutral, to a feeling above neutral. This is why I call it F.U.N. journaling. F.U.N. standing for: Feelings Under Neutral. Also my hope is that it's fun and empowering to do. It is for me and people I've helped use it. In fact, I often find myself laughing while doing it because the fear-based emotions I'm listening to can actually sound silly sometimes.

It's like, "Oh really fear? Tell me more about how all my closest friends are going to laugh at me."

As Cher Horowitz would say, "As if!"

This process I work with was inspired by teachings from Gabrielle Bernstein, Wayne Dyer and Marianne Williamson. I'm sure many other teachers share similar techniques as well.

This is very powerful and something a hero must do daily. The better you get at it, the easier it will be to flow through this process *without* having to take time out to journal; but that may take months or years so don't give up.

I no longer need to journal out every single emotion that's below neutral as I can flow through the scale pretty easily these days, but if something is really difficult for me I still write out this process.

Here's a glimpse at how it works. Below I've filled in an example of a F.U.N. journal entry using another specific feeling I'm going through that's below neutral on the chart: I'm afraid I won't be able to finish this book in an organized way by the time it's due. Here's how the F.U.N. journaling helps:

Step 1:
Say hi to your fear-based emotion and lovingly welcome it in.

Hey there fear of finishing this book on time, welcome in! I'm ready to listen and work with you.

Step 2:
Ask it: "What message do you have for me?" - In other words, what fear-based belief/old story is popping up right now?

"You're too distracted. You'll never be able to concisely say what you need to by your publishing date."

Step 3:
Ask yourself: "What does this tell me about what I really desire?"

This must mean I desire to feel like my message is concise & flows from me easily and in an organized and timely way.

Step 4:
Thank your fear for giving you more clarity about your desires & the direction you want to go.

Thank you so much fear for helping me get clear on this goal to be more concise and in flow!

Step 5:
Write a statement of willingness to change your beliefs using this new data.

I am willing to change this belief. I'm willing to see myself organized and to feel like my message flows easily.

Step 6:
Write out the new belief you are ready to exchange the answer to step 2 with.

"I know exactly what I'm writing and the order in which I'm writing it. I feel it flowing through me in the easiest, quickest way now. I will easily be ready in time!"

Did you notice that in my example I expressed appreciation to the below-neutral emotion?

That's such a powerful step in this process of working with your feelings under neutral as a total cham-

Super Intense

pion: thank them! Be grateful for every emotion you feel that's below neutral once you have used it to propel you forward.

I used to think I had to forgive all of my lower emotions, but then I realized that finding genuine gratitude for them was much more powerful. The definition of forgiveness is to cease feeling resentment. By nature, when you can feel true appreciation for something, you automatically must let go of resentment. Feeling true thankfulness for your emotions transforms them, and you. I am thankful for every fear, anxiety and belief of unworthiness. I'm thankful for all the pain those emotions have ever caused. Thanks to them I better understand what I truly desire in this life. They have guided and shaped me. As they have you.

Every hero was shaped in some way by something most would consider "bad." For Tony Stark, after an explosion caused shrapnel to enter his body and he was given an electromagnet from terrorists trying to keep him alive to build them weapons, he could have just given in to how "bad" that situation was. Instead, it motivated him. It inspired him to create the Arc Reactor in his chest that eventually powers his Ironman suits.

For you, your intense feelings of despair and unworthiness can lead to creating your own version of an Ironman suit. It can lead you to pursue unique dreams and visions that no one else has. It can help you become the hero version of yourself you've always known was living within you.

To do this, after finding that appreciation, use the feeling below neutral's message for you to create a new belief. If your feeling is telling you: "You're not good enough and you'll never succeed." Well we can find appreciation for this feeling because it's helping us gain clarity on the fact that we desire to feel like we're good enough and that we already are successful. We can now _become willing to believe_ that we are worthy, successful humans.

Being _willing to believe_ this new belief is huge. Especially if you've been stuck in the old belief for so long. That old belief may keep coming back up for quite a while. But as you lean into your willingness to transform it, it begins to transform.

This is why fear - and every other emotion below neutral - is for champions. These emotions help you rise like a phoenix from the ashes. These feelings are gifts, as long as you use them.

Here's a step-by-step explanation of the F.U.N. journaling process. I encourage you to work through this process with at least one feeling below neutral daily, if not more.

Six Steps to Use Your Intense Emotions Under Neutral for Good!

F.U.N. Journaling

Step 1: Say "hi" to your fear-based emotion (your Feeling Under Neutral) and welcome it in.

Step 2: Ask the emotion: "what message do you have for me?" - really let yourself listen to whatever fear-based story this emotion is telling you. Be open to hearing it, without judging it.

Step 3: Ask yourself: "what does this teach me about what I really desire?" Hint: It's usually that you desire the opposite of the message from Step 2.

Step 4: Thank you Feeling Under Neutral for giving you more clarity about your desires and the direction you want to go. This emotion has been guiding you, and you finally listened. It's time to express your appreciation. (Thank yourself for listening while you're at it!)

Step 5: Become willing to change the belief you wrote down in Step 2. Write a statement of your willingness to change your belief.

Step 6: Use your desires from Step 3, to purposefully choose and write down a *new belief* to replace the one you uncovered in Step 2.

Step 1:
Say hi to your fear-based emotion and lovingly welcome it in.

Step 2:
Ask it: "What message do you have for me?" - In other words, what fear-based belief/old story is popping up right now?

Step 3:
Ask yourself: "What does this tell me about what I really desire?"

Step 4:
Thank your fear for giving you more clarity about your desires & the direction you want to go.

Step 5:
Write a statement of willingness to change your beliefs using this new data.

Step 6:
Write out the new belief you are ready to exchange the answer to step 2 with.

CHAPTER 11: MIRROR, MIRROR

You ever find yourself in the same situations over and over again? You're constantly attracting a romantic partner who takes you for granted? Or you're continually ending up in low paying jobs that wear your down?

It's because the world around us is a reflection of what's happening within us.

This is a beautiful thing.

The situations we are going through are indicators of the lessons we must uncover within ourselves. Everything that is around us is a mirror to us in some way.

Once we recognize that we can see how helpful what we're going through really is!

It's not just the situations that happen on repeat

that are our mirrors. Every little thing is. From the friend who is super needy, to the beautiful flowers you pass on you walk every day.

Nothing is without its purpose and once we learn the lesson and work on healing our inner landscape, then our outer world can start to change. We do this through changing beliefs using the F.U.N. journaling.

I mentioned the boss I had who would scream at me in Chapter 7. In that situation, even after I learned how to work through that and keep my inner peace, I still kept ending up in situations where people I worked with would yell at or take advantage of me.

I had to figure out, what the heck was happening inside of me that caused that to be what was in the world around me?

Through the F.U.N. journaling, I uncovered that I had a belief that I wasn't good enough. I also believed that if I spoke up and defended myself that things would just be harder for me.

I had to rewrite that reality and see that I could stand up for myself with love - not in a way that belittles anyone else, but in a way that lovingly empowers *me*. When I finally recognized this and set boundaries in a kind but firm way three years ago, I haven't found myself in a situation like that since.

Here's how you use the world around you as your mirror to learn more about yourself.

1. F.U.N. journaling: Use it to look at the people in your life who bother you; the situations that just keep reoccuring; the drama you're trying to escape. Take out your journal now and practice one F.U.N. journalling around one of these scenarios. Keep it out for the next step.
2. Beliefs gratitude list: Your world is also mirroring to you all the great beliefs inside of you. Celebrate that. If you have a friend that is there for you no matter what, it demonstrates that a part of you believes you are worthy of such loving, unconditional support. Now make a header in your journal that says "Beliefs Gratitude List" and show appreciation for all the beliefs that are making your life great. See an example below.

This also helps you to practice equality, oneness and connection with the world around you, as discussed in the next chapter. Recognizing that everyone and everything around you is somehow mirroring to you your thoughts and beliefs helps you to see how everything is interconnected. We can better appreciate the people and situations in our lives that basically just seem to suck.

They don't just suck!

They also serve.

But they only serve when we do the work. Use your F.U.N. journaling to get to the bottom of any stressful emotional situation. As your beliefs change, so will the world around you. Enjoy this game!

Here's an example of my current "Beliefs Gratitude List" to give you some ideas of how to do this:

Beliefs Gratitude List Example

I am grateful for the belief that...

I am loved

I am supported

It's safe to be myself

I am creative

My creative visions are possible

It's possible for me to follow my dreams

The perfect path for me is continually unfolding

I am confident in the direction I'm headed

The world around me is beautiful

I love and appreciate these beliefs. I am grateful that I

feel this way. Thank you, beliefs, for serving me. I see you in the world around me in the form of family and friends who love and support me; opportunities to express myself creatively unfolding before me; and beautiful displays in nature all around me. These beliefs are serving me and I celebrate them.

CHAPTER 12: WE ARE EQUALS

This is a trick I practice daily to improve my ability to use my intensity for good and it totally rocks.

It's super easy too.

A lot of times our fears and anxieties relate to seeing differences in people. You see someone experiencing homelessness and you feel pity - perhaps even guilt. You go to a concert and feel like you'll never be as good or as important as the person you look up to.

While sometimes it's useful to compare ourselves to others because it helps us determine the direction we want to head in life and how we want to show up - because of social media, comparison and separation are running rampant. You're expending so much unnecessary energy seeing differences and experiencing emotions about those differences.

Whether it's because we think someone is better than us, or worse off than us, we're constantly creating divides with our minds that cause emotional discomfort in one form or another.

If you're trying to get a handle on your intense nature, why add extra flame to the fire when it doesn't serve you?

...I just realized that's not the phrase...it's fuel to the fire, right? Whatever, you know what I mean.

It's a way of draining your emotional greatness. Almost every time you compare yourself or judge another you're wasting your beautiful powers.

It's time to better control your powers so you can use them more wisely.

Here's the trick that helps me avoid utilizing my powers wastefully in these situations: see everyone as equal and connected.

Besides the fact that we may have all come from one initial singularity when our Universe was created (which *really* ties us together), here's a few steps I like to use to get to a feeling of oneness:

1. Return to choosing not to label something as good or bad. You don't know the whole story ever, so why judge it?

2. Do a time crunch: Modern humans have been around for 200,000 years. At least according to the best evidence science has found so far. That sounds like a really long time, to *us*. But if you were to convert the Earth's history into a 12 month span, those 200,000 years become the last hour of the last day of the year. So, relatively speaking - and everything is relative - let yourself take the scope that 200,000 years is not that long ago, especially given Earth's 4.5 billion year history.
3. Remember that at that time, we were all related and connected in some way. As time went on our genetic lines grew more distanced but we can ALL trace our lines back to common African ancestors - well if we had enough information. But for now at the very least we do know all human life as we know it started in Africa 200,000 years ago. Our ancestors, every single one of us, all started their lives in the same place.
4. See that connection in everyone you meet. We're all just very distant family. Instead of feeling separation, when we lean into the fact that we all come from the same place, we can have greater appreciation of the people around us. We're all just figuring out life in these human bodies.
5. If that isn't enough, you can continue to choose to see everyone as children as dis-

cussed in the next chapter. This often dissolves barriers and welcomes in connection.

6. If you're open to spirituality, you can use your beliefs to help you see equality and connection. What I personally choose to believe to help me see oneness is that a loving energy of the Universe animates all of us - that it's the truth behind each of us. No matter what the physical bodies are doing, beneath that what ls flowing through us all is unconditional love that we're all connected to. I choose to see things that way (as well as the previously listed ways in the steps above) because it simply makes me feel good and helps me dissolve judgement and barriers. This reduces the amount of energy I waste on emotions tied to judgement, such as anxiety and fear.

You don't have to have any spiritual beliefs to see oneness and equality. You can just make the choice to see every human as an equally worthy being and watch how you save so much time and energy on the emotions that come with judging others and creating separation.

The power of we

Once you start seeing everyone as equal, your beliefs about yourself start becoming your beliefs about others too, and vice versa. This, in my experience, has the power of amplifying the belief.

In addition to believing that *I* am loved and worthy, I can see and feel that we *all* are loved and worthy.

Each affirmation and positive belief I have for myself can be amplified by seeing it in others.

Give it a try.

Get out your journal and look at your "Beliefs Gratitude List" from the last chapter. Take one or more of those beliefs and spend a moment exploring what it feels like to believe it for everyone, not just yourself.

Replace the word "I" with the word "we."

Do you feel a difference?

"We are loved."

"We are supported."

"We are free to pursue our dreams."

I like to explore this feeling when walking by strangers on the street. Whatever uplifting belief I'm currently focused on, I imagine it extending to them as well.

For example, if I'm on a walk and I'm focused on how free I feel, I think in my mind "we are so free" everytime I pass someone. For me, it lets my sensitive and intense nature take the wheel in the most uplifting way.

Go out there and give it a try!

CHAPTER 13: THE CHILD TRICK

Seeing the people we struggle to be around and the emotions we desire to avoid as small, scared children, is one of the greatest "tricks" you can use to instantly soften the situation and choose to see it with love. You can even do it with public figures that annoy you.

When we encounter a human in a fully grown body we usually assume they're 100% emotionally mature and responsible people. But that describes, like, very few people. Very few.

When you act out, is it something you're proud of?

No one is!

Everyone is doing the best they can, just like when we were children.

In second grade this kid would throw rocks and

money - yes, you read that right, rock and money - to get me to like him. Since he was a kid we laugh it off because we know he must have genuinely thought that was the best way to get my attention. We know it wasn't the most romantic move, and actually a sign of toxic masculinity - but we are comfortable accepting the fact that he likely didn't know better.

We assume the second people enter their adult bodies all of a sudden they know better. If they were never explicitly taught, why would they randomly know better?

When I was working in education I can remember thinking that telling a young person not to run down the hall because they "know better" was a legitimate way to guide them in the right action. When my mentor was like, "how do we know if they actually do know better?" I realized how often I make assumptions about people's actions.

We all do.

It takes time to learn appropriate behaviors. Instead of assuming one knows better, *show the way.*

This goes with people *and* emotions.

Often times our scared emotions are really just like scared children who do not know any better. They think everyone will laugh at you if you show yourself for who you really are. They believe you could never find true love and will always be alone. They have all sorts of limiting beliefs and need _you_ to be the adult who holds their hand and shows them the truth. Since you are in charge of your beliefs, you must help guide them to new ones.

It's hard to do that when we belittle other people or our emotions for being "bad." When you instead view them as small scared children, genuinely trying their best, it becomes a lot easier.

CHAPTER 14: YOU ARE YOUR BEST GUIDE

For so long I sought all the answers outside of myself.

I often still do, even though I know better.

It just seems like it'd be so much easier. Can't someone just tell me the meaning of life already? Come on!!

But everytime I look outside myself, someone else has an idea for me that's based on what's best for them. Someone else always thinks they know what's best.

This is why I've said it before and I'll say it again: I *don't* know what's best. I'm just sharing what works for me, in hopes you can find what works for you. **You** must become your own best expert.

I will tell you that when I need guidance, it best

comes from me, because now I know how to listen.

This might be counterintuitive because if I need guidance, doesn't that mean I don't have it?

Here's the thing - we only *think* we don't know what's best for us. Through meditation and centeredness we can get clear and receive the guidance we need.

It's like all of a sudden you'll just start to understand these knowings within you. This becomes a superpower in and of itself.

Instead of being wishy washy about how, why and what you should do next, you'll just know.

How much of your emotional pain comes from being indecisive or unsure about what's best for you?

Wouldn't it be nice to have clarity?

A big part of the equation to living as a superhero with emotional sensitivity and intensity is no longer wasting your emotional energy on indecisiveness and uncertainty.

Or at least not doing it *as much*.

This inner guidance muscle is your intuition. We often ignore it and try to use logic instead, but our inner guidance knows so much more than logic.

You know how teachers always suggest to go with the first answer you think is right on multiple choice tests? That's a commonly used and accepted form of trusting intuition.

When I first started building this muscle, I just barely was learning how to trust listening to my gut. So I made a promise to myself to follow whatever guidance I thought I was receiving, no matter how silly it seemed. One day before work I had an impulse to grab a hair tie. I remember logic coming into my head and saying "you don't need one, your hair is already up." Since I was committed to listening to my inner guidance I grabbed the hair tie anyway. Almost the entire day went by and then, just before leaving work, a co-worker said she needed a hair tie. Voila. A super simple example of how listening to your intuition can help you despite the thinking brain trying to rationalize against it.

It may have been a silly situation, but that's good. It's good to test this first with the small, less important things. It's like lifting weights, or so I assume...I don't lift weights. But presumably, when people get started they don't just start by deadlifting 300lbs on day one.

Just like EVERY other thing we're doing - this takes time and practice. You gotta do the reps to build your intuition muscles. But once you get them nice and strong you will 100% notice a difference.

Here are some of the inner-guidance workouts I recommend you add to your super-human training:

1. The blind drive/walk

Okay, so don't just put on a blindfold and go for a walk or a drive. Please, don't do that. But *do* go for a walk or a drive, somewhere safe of course, without any agenda. Let yourself get a sense of which direction your intuition wants you to go: "left," "right," "straight." Just listen and feel for the directions and see what happens. Another way to do this is if you have a daily drive that takes you somewhere familiar- work, school, home - and there are multiple ways to get there, just listen and feel for whether or not to turn left or right or go straight when you're presented with those options.

When I first started experimenting with this I questioned myself because I had listened to my intuition and ended up in horrible traffic. Just as I was ready to give up on trusting my intuition, thanks to that traffic I caught something I needed to hear on the radio that I would have missed if I had gone the other way.

We often don't know why we receive certain guidance until later. Let yourself be curious with this and experiment.

Important note about this technique: Only do this when you have extra time to spare. If you're in a rush and are stressed about time, you won't be able to accurately hear and feel your intuition right away. As the muscle grows you can practice this even when you're pressed for time, but right off the bat I recommend only doing it when you're free to take your time.

2. The yes/no ab workout

This one is fun. Way more fun than actual ab workouts in my opinion.

You can do this with all sorts of things, but to start, sit in a quiet place and take a few deep breaths. If it helps you to focus, close your eyes. Bring all of your awareness in on your lower abdomen and ask your body: "Is my name ___?" Fill in the blank with someone else's name. Then try again with your actual name. See if you you can start to feel what a "yes" and a "no" feels like in your body.

Once you think you can feel the answer, try more workouts. Grab a book and with your eyes closed, flip to a page. Ask yourself: "is this page number X?" Just use a random number and see if you can feel a "yes" or a "no" answer. Then check yourself.

You can practice this with all sorts of yes or no questions. Get creative and practice often. The more you learn what a "yes" and a "no" feels like in your body, the easier it is to make decisions in your life.

3. The daily hits journal

You already have a bunch of intuitive hits every day. These are the moments when you just "know" something is right. When you meet that new friend and you have this deep inner feeling that you're just going to hit it off right away. Or when you start driving and have this sense you forgot something, only to discover when you get to where you're headed that you left your water bottle sitting on the counter.

Take note of these every day. Highlight them. The more you point them out, the better you get at recognizing them. The better you get at recognizing them, the more of them you start to notice.

Make a daily log and watch your skills grow.

4. The silence bump

This one's fantastic for if you're all caught up in a thinking frenzy and don't know what advice or opinions to trust. This happens to me all the time, so I use this trick often. You'll want to block off 20 min to make this work. For a guided version of this go to www.marisaimon.com/freemeditations and look for "Receiving Guidance."

Here's how it works: Find a quiet space to sit where you will not be interrupted. I like to have something to rest my back against, but if you don't have that do your best to sit up straight either way. Place your hands in your lap facing downwards and close your eyes.

Take three deep inhales through your nose and out through your mouth to center in. After that just breathe regularly.

Focus on your breath, or even an ambient sound in the room like the air conditioner. Just give your mind something to center in on. As thoughts emerge, do not judge them or hold on to them, just let them flow and continually return your awareness to your breath.

Eventually the thoughts will slow.

Eventually your body will start to feel light.

Eventually you'll start to feel very peaceful.

And finally, even if for only 30 seconds, you'll start to feel clarity and inspiration.

Just welcome it in and do not get hung up on it. Just let it be.

When you're ready, slowly bring your awareness back to the room around you. You'll notice that you feel more centered and you may be inspired to do something. It may appear to be COMPLETELY unrelated to the problem you were facing, but just trust it and go with it.

The more you practice building your intuition muscles, the stronger they get and the easier life becomes. Have fun with this and celebrate your wins.

Marisa Imon

Know it takes time and never give up.

CHAPTER 15: PUT YOURSELF FIRST

Hey there dear hero,

I know you want to rip your heart out to save the lives of others, but that isn't how this works.

You having a harder life doesn't make someone's easier - and even if it does, it can never be a long-term solution. You will burn out.

And then you're useless.

I used to think that I had to work near the poverty level of the community I was serving in order to really connect and be of service. So I spent a couple of years in AmeriCorps doing just that.

I thought that if I was wealthy, I'd be doing a disservice to all the people who were struggling.

For some reason I just could not see the value in me

being taken care of. It was like, if I'm here to help others, then I just need to sacrifice and do what I gotta do.

But that thinking is wildly flawed.

Just because you have more doesn't mean others have to have less.

Just because you take time to yourself doesn't mean others get less help.

When I gave and gave of myself as a non-profit youth worker, I may have been of service to the lives I touched, but what I also managed to do was destroy my physical, mental and emotional health along the way. In only a few short years of overworking to try to be as helpful to the world as I possibly could be, I suddenly wasn't very useful anymore.

I mentally, emotionally and physically couldn't keep up.

To be sustainably helpful on this planet, YOU must come before everyone else.

You must make yourself your number one priority.

What good are you to others if you don't do this?

I get pushback on this sometimes. We need to change the culture around this. We do it on airplanes (always put your mask on first), so why is it so hard to do it in our daily life. When it comes to setting an example, shouldn't we want others to learn how to have healthy boundaries and self-care practices?

When you set aside time for your self care, you are more effective at being of service.

When you set boundaries on what you can and cannot do, you are more effective at the things you *do* do.

(ha, do do)

If you want to be a hero, you must be a hero to yourself first. Period.

This means putting your opinions about yourself before the opinions others have of you.

No one's opinions of you have anything to do with you. This is why it's so important you know who you are inside and out. No one else can sway you if you put yourself first. If you make loving and honoring yourself your priority, it doesn't matter what anyone else thinks. Their opinions say more about them than they do you.

Take a moment to get your journal out and answer these questions:

What commitment has been weighing me down?

Where am I overextending myself?

Who's opinion about me have I let affect me negatively?

What's one tiny step I can make to improve this today?

△△△

That's it. It doesn't have to be all the changes all at once but if you get honest with yourself daily about the areas where you are overextending yourself and commit to just one tiny step to improve your situation, over time it adds up.

Whatever you recognize can be done to improve your situation - do it! Why wait? If you want to be a hero, practice on yourself.

The next two chapters are dedicated to ways you can do this.

CHAPTER 16: SLEEP, YOU IDIOT

I used to think sleep was the worst - how dare it get in the way of my exciting brain activity!? Now, I realized if I don't sleep, then *I'm* the worst...

Kudos to you if you're already a pro at sleeping every night and feel refreshed every morning. If you're already making this a priority, feel free to skip this chapter.

If you're not, read this chapter so I can kick your butt into doing it - and give you the tools that helped a helpless insomniac, yours truly, learn how to sleep again.

I know what it's like to be an insomniac that cannot be put out by even the heaviest duty pills. The doctor's tried everything. Either they made me feel horrible and didn't put me to sleep. Or they'd make me trip and think I was sleeping. For the latter, I'd almost always wake up to find out I had been crafting all night long.

To this day I don't know exactly what triggered my manic episode - whether it was the extra energy from mania, or the lack of sleep from insomnia. The two were a vicious cycle that fueled each other. I have a suspicion that if I had actually slept like a regular human during that time in my life, then it would have never led to clinical insanity.

It doesn't matter how much I meditate, how often I look at my fears with love through exercises like F.U.N. journaling, or how true I am to myself - if I don't give my body the sleep it needs, I will fail at using my intensity for good. Period. In fact, I suck at handling any emotion when I'm sleep deprived. And I can't imagine you're any different. Yes, some people need fewer hours than others, but *everyone* needs it.

Sleep deprivation leads to erratic mood swings and difficulty thinking. These are very important situations to avoid when you're learning how to wield your power.

If you don't practice anything else I'm offering in this book, at least do this.

Insomnia often goes hand-in-hand with other emotional illnesses, which makes a lot of sense. Sometimes it feels like a never-ending vicious cycle because the anxiety and depression keep you awake and the sleeplessness exacerbates the emotional pain.

I *never* would have thought that one day I'd be getting into bed by 8pm, and totally loving it, but it ended up being exactly what I needed.

The bedtime I should have had but never followed in my childhood and teenage years is the bedtime I adopted when I committed to getting well. I'd turn off electronics an hour before bed and ensure that I was under the covers with at least an hour before I'd have to fall asleep to get a full 8 hours. *This means I'd get in bed with at least nine hours before wake-up time and with no electronics in sight.*

Adopt this plan now...please:

Step 1: Electronic off and away at least nine hours before wake-up time. Ideally you can hide your phone in a drawer in kitchen or somewhere else far enough away that it won't be easy to get up in get it.

Step 2: Prepare your bedside with the following items:

- **Journal:** I recommend always ending your day with F.U.N. journaling and gratitude lists from Chapter 10 and daily hits list from Chapter 14.
- **Coloring Books:** Keep coloring books with crayons by your bedside and color as you're waiting to get sleepy (word of caution: I use crayons not only because I love them, but also if you

fall asleep while using them, they can't stab you like a box of loose colored pencils in your sheets will, or bleed everywhere like pens will…trust me, I'm speaking from experience)

- **Brain Teasers:** Keep puzzle books (sudoku, logic puzzles, crossword puzzles, etc.) by your bedside and do those as you're drifting off. Trust me, if you're trying to figure out a logic puzzle before bed, your brain will definitely start to wear down! Did you ever fall asleep doing homework? Same thing, but more fun!

- **Meditation:** Obviously, this is a no-brainer. The only catch here is you want to do your own instead of listening to one on YouTube or from a playlist, unless you have a CD. This is to avoid using your phone or computer which can instantly drag you down a rabbit hole if you see a notification. If you must use electronics you can do an evening meditation or a sleep journey from my free meditations: www.marisaimon.com/freemeditations - just put your phone or computer on do not disturb.

- **Books:** This is so obvious I almost didn't put it here, but we all know having a book to read before bed can help you drift off. Be sure not to choose something so gripping that you can't put it down, or so scary that you can't turn off your lights.

Step 3: Practice this while falling asleep

- **Body Relaxation:** A very simple meditation you

can do on your own is to envision a wave of light slowly rolling over you from head to toe, relaxing each and every muscle (even cheeks, elbows, fingers and anything else you don't normally think of relaxing). As you see this light touching each muscle, let go of any tension you're holding there. You'll be surprised how many muscles you'll likely be clenching when you lie down. This helps you deliberately relax each and every muscle. By the time you reach your toes your eyelids will feel like they are glued shut.

- **Counting Good Things:** List things you are grateful for in your head instead of counting sheep. Just start rambling with something you're grateful for and keep listing more and more until you fall asleep. It's just like counting sheep but way more rewarding. This list can start with something as simple as your pillows.

Here are some other general tips:
- Use a sunrise simulator to wake you up in the morning. These will gradually wake you over the course of 30 minutes using a light that simulates the sun rising through your window so that your body can gently rise without being harshly awoken by the sound of an alarm. Tip: Most of these also do timed "sunsets" so that you can have the light on for an hour and it will gradually darken as you're falling asleep. That way you don't have to disturb your sleepiness by reaching for a light switch.

- Put your phone on Do Not Disturb during "electronics off" time. Even if you're hiding it in the kitchen.
- Put something in front of any digital clock in the room to block the light from displaying the time. The last thing you need is almost being asleep only to notice that you've been trying to fall asleep for over an hour. That will instantly get you back up and ruminating about how hard it is it to sleep.
- In your meditation space during the day, take time to visualize yourself falling asleep easily and waking up rested. Allow yourself to feel the happiness this would bring you as if it was already true for you. This will help you start attracting easier, sounder sleep. If you believe you can you sleep well, you will.
- Watch your language! If you so much as utter the phrase "I'm a light sleeper" or "I have a hard time falling asleep" or "I never get enough rest," then you are setting yourself up for failure because you are putting out the energy to attract more of what you're complaining about. If you wanna sleep, but you can't, don't feed energy into not being able to sleep or you make it infinitely harder on yourself. Remember how the world is a mirror of our inner landscape? You being unable to sleep is also connected to a belief that you can't. No need to help that belief get stronger.
- Adopt a sleepy and cuddly pet. This last one

is kind of a joke, but not. It makes the list because it worked for me, completely by accident. If you're not ready for a pet, don't adopt one. However, if you already have been considering adopting one anyway, going to a local rescue center and asking for a pet that likes to cuddle and sleep with its owner could be a godsend. I adopted my American Staffordshire Terrier, Jordan, (who LOVES to sleep and has the cutest, most relaxing deep breathing when he does) about one week after I started seriously trying to reclaim my sleep schedule. If I wasn't in bed by 8pm, Jordan would jump on my pillows and take my spot. He trained me to get to bed in time (because if I didn't, I would have to fight him for my pillow) and his gentle breathing and perfect cuddling accelerated my ability to fall asleep every night. I know this is probably totally out of the question for many people, but I feel like it's worth mentioning since Jordan totally changed my life (in many ways) and still helps me sleep soundly every night...Except for when he accidentally kicks me during a particularly active dream.

CHAPTER 17: MORNING AND EVENING ROUTINES

A big part of being a superhero is self-care. You can't serve anyone if you don't serve yourself and a big chunk of this is setting specific time to yourself each day. A common way to do this is by setting morning and evening routines.

Morning and evening routines are exactly as they sound. You've likely been doing one anyway, but perhaps it hasn't been intentional. Maybe your evening routine is scrolling through Facebook until you fall asleep, or passing out to whatever is on TV. Perhaps you're waking up each morning to the sound of a blaring alarm that makes you angry that you're awake and so your routine is to hit snooze a million times.

Let's start with the evening routine because really, **a good morning routine starts with a good evening routine.**

Take a second and get real with yourself. *What is your current routine or lack of one like?* Is it lifting you up? Is it making you feel loved - especially by yourself?

If it's not, let's change that. Here's a few wonderful ways to unwind. If you're busy, know that incorporating at least one of these does not take away from the rest of your life. If you need permission because you feel guilty doing this for yourself, not only do you have permission, but I'm ordering you to at least do something kind to yourself before bed. If you really want to be a superhero, you must come first.

Here's some great ways to get started:

Pampering/Honoring Your body:

In addition to the methods for falling sleep mentioned in the previous chapter, you can incorporate some beautiful self-care practices around pampering yourself. These can be things like taking an epsom salt bath, changing into jammies that make you feel happy, and applying deliciously scented lotions or essential oils while you listen to relaxing music.

Take time to *honor* your body and feel love for yourself as you prepare to unwind and fall asleep. As you bath your body, or put lotion on your skin, say "I love you" to every part of your body that you touch. Feel gratitude for each and every cell. Be present in the moment with your body as you unwind.

This body is what enables you to share your superpowers with the world. Treat it as such. Pampering before bed is always a good idea.

Journaling

By now I hope you're already at least F.U.N. journaling at the end of the day, but there's other ways to use your journal at the end of the day as well:

- Write yourself a letter of appreciation. You are doing a lot of work and making some big changes. Tell yourself what a great job you're doing.
- List out everything causing you to feel grateful at this moment. It can be as seemingly insignificant as being grateful for the paper you are writing on or as big as being grateful to have just graduated college. It doesn't matter how big or small. In the scheme of things, they are all important to recognize and appreciate.
- Write out a dream you have for your life as if it already happened. Imagine you just landed your dream job, or you just moved into your dream home. What does it feel like? What does it look like? Write every detail in present tense and just

have fun with it. Don't get caught up in how it could happen. That part doesn't matter. Just enjoy the feeling of it.

Intention-Setting

This practice is beautiful because A. it takes like zero extra time, and B. it can have a pretty big impact - especially if done continually over time.

When I was super little - like maybe four or five - a babysitter told me I could choose what I dreamed about and control my dreams. I chose Bugs Bunny, of course. He told me that the way you do it is to think about what you want to dream about every night until you see it in your dreams. Then, once it happens in your dreams you'll be able to know you're dreaming. I now know this to be lucid dreaming but when I was a kid I just knew it as hanging out with Bugs. It totally worked!

Sure enough, not only do I let myself take control of my dreams whenever I need to (I usually don't unless I get scared in a dream, then I remind myself it's a dream and change in the topic) I also use my dreams as additional guidance in my life.

Not all the times - sometimes I don't remember any dreams from the night before and other times I have no clue what they mean - but I know for sure that if I set an intention enough nights in a row asking to get clarity around something in my life, eventually the dreams give great guidance.

All you have to do is say, out loud or in your mind, "while I dream tonight, I welcome in guidance around X" and fill in the blank with whatever it is you need help around. This is important, also set the intention to remember the message upon awakening. If you don't you might get the message and then just have a vague memory that doesn't help you as clearly.

You can also set the intention to wake up rested, or to fall asleep peacefully, or to let go of a topic you're holding onto while you sleep. Sleep is a lot more productive than we give it credit for!

Meditation

As mentioned in the previous chapter, meditation is a great way to fall asleep. If you're doing this evening routine within an hour of bedtime, try to avoid using your electronics for meditation. If you must, make sure it's on "do not disturb" or airplane mode and try to use an app or wear the glasses that block blue light. If you do use your phone or computer you can use my evening meditations found on my website at www.marisaimon.com/freemeditations

Otherwise, here's a suggested meditation practice:

- Sit in a quiet space where you will not be interrupted, with hands in lap facing downward and gently close your eyes.
- Take three deep cleansing breaths in through the

nose and out through the mouth and then return to regularly-paced breathing.
- Focus in on your breath: As you breathe in, focus on pushing out your lower abdomen, and let it contract on every exhale. This really slows the body down and tells it it's time to unwind.
- Let yourself now imagine an anchor dropping down from your sit bones and anchoring you to the Earth. Really let yourself feel grounded as you breathe deeply.
- Imagine a bucket over your head full of white light pouring down over you, washing over your head, shoulders, torso and legs - all the way down to your feet. Feel this liquid light washing away anything from the day that you're ready to let go of.
- Once you see the bucket as empty, focus in on your heart and let a sense of appreciation build and you think about your gratitude for the day.
- Finally, set an intention for the rest of the evening and when your ready, slowly open your eyes.

Now let's talk about your morning.

Gone are the mornings of waking up to an annoying buzzing sound, the rush of getting ready, turning on TV to listen to the news, or hitting snooze a million times over.

Any method of waking that doesn't allow you to start your day in peace ends today.

From now on you commit to a better way. My favorite and easiest way to wake up peacefully, suggested in the previous chapter, is a sunrise simulator. This slowly lights the room, tricking your brain into thinking the sun woke you up even if you live in a climate where the sun doesn't rise until hours after your desired waking time.

There are also sound machines that will slowly awaken you to peaceful music or nature sounds.

I've used several apps that have you sleep with your phone by your side in the bed to monitor your sleep and wake you at the perfect time for you.

Of all of the above methods, the sunrise simulator works best for me. *Find what works for you*, but know that the phone sleep apps do take away the added benefit of going to sleep in an electronic-free environment.

When you have your ideal method of waking, set it for *at least* 10 minutes earlier than the start of all of the distractions in your home environment. For example, if you have a busy morning of getting showered, doing your hair and make-up and feel rushed with only two hours to get ready, give yourself two hours and ten minutes. You want these extra ten minutes before the "craziness" of the day begins so that you don't feel rushed.

Once you have that minimum of ten minutes

carved out for you, and you have your wonderfully relaxing way of waking up, then it's time to choose what you want to do as you wake up.

No matter what you choose, always start with gratitude. Here is my simple suggestion for a morning routine that works wonders and can be done in less than ten minutes.

The nice thing about only needing ten minutes is that you can do this while you're still in bed! A lot of times my morning routine just looks like I'm sleeping in. It's fantastic!

So, you can start while you're still in bed, and just waking up. You may not have even fully opened your eyes yet and that's okay. Begin by expressing gratitude for the fact that you are alive for another day - not everyone woke up this morning. Feel appreciation for your life and for the body you are in. Let it stretch as you focus on how beautiful it is to be alive in this body.

Say in your mind: "Thank you!"

And take a few moments to just focus on your breath. You can sit up in bed to do this, actually get up and go to an area to meditate - or just do it while still lying down.

Have no agenda with this. Just focus on your breath and be.

When you're ready to wrap this up, begin to shift

your awareness to an intention for the day. This can be inspired by a question from Chapter 18 or anything else on your mind. Set the intention by saying it out loud or in your mind, or even better, by writing it in your journal. Once you're clear on it, say thank you as if your intention already came true and let yourself feel like it really is. I mean, if you create your reality anyway, *why not let it feel like your intention has already come to pass?*

Some of my favorite daily intentions:
- Today is the best day of my life so far!
- I welcome in creative ways for everything to work out perfectly today.
- I flow through the day in the funnest way.

As an added bonus, end by heading to your mirror, looking in your eyes and saying an affirmation to yourself that feels encouraging. This could be as simple as three words: "I love you." You could also say to yourself, "thank you for committing to this work. I am proud of you." This may feel a bit uncomfortable, but that's okay. Stretch beyond your comfort zone a little bit here and give yourself some love. The more you commit to this, the more comfortable it becomes to look yourself in the eyes lovingly and provide yourself with guidance and support. Tell yourself that you got this; that you are here for yourself.

Commit to this simple routine (or another peaceful routine of your own design) for a week and watch how this simple shift makes a world of a difference. You'll be less interested in watching news that just causes stress (if you still want morning news in a non-stressful way I recommend the daily 10-min podcast, *The NewsWorthy*). You'll be less pulled into the dramas of people around you in the morning, less attracted to unhealthy foods for breakfast and better able to see creative solutions for bringing peace to every aspect of your morning.

Did you notice that nowhere in this morning routine did I say grab your phone and read your emails? Wait to grab your phone or hop on your computer until after your 10-minute morning routine is done. At the least.

Create a morning deserving of a superhero. Because you are one.

Journal Time:

Go ahead and take a moment now to get out your journal and set an intention for how you want your mornings and evenings to look. **What's one simple change you can commit to today?** Even though ideally you'll try out the full morning routine for a week - you don't have to change everything overnight. You could just, for now, commit to waking up by feeling appreciation *before* reaching for your phone, but do commit to at least one simple switch to get started. Write down your game plan in your journal now.

CHAPTER 18: HELPFUL QUESTIONS

We're only as good as the questions we ask.

And so often, our questions suck.

Our heads are constantly full of questions like:
"Why doesn't he like me?"
"How come I never get ahead?"
"Why am I so fat?"
"Why can't I make enough money?"
"How come she gets to have it so good and I don't?"

Almost all the questions we ask put us in victim mode and take away our power. We're almost always asking why things aren't going right, instead of how they can be better.

Think about some of the questions you've had today.

Maybe you're not even aware of them yet. Take inventory this week and just be aware. Don't judge yourself, just notice when you have a question that's guiding you and pay attention to how it feels.

I have a very specific example of how this impacted my life.

In 2018 I was guided by the question: "how can I make more money?"

I was so stressed out and worried about my business I just wanted to know: "how can I make money?"

Because that was my guiding question, I found myself in dozens of opportunities to make money - none of them in ways I love.

Our questions guide us, whether we realize it or not. With that question I was guided to all sorts of multi-level marketing companies that pitched the promise of boatloads of passive income. I romanticized them all - then realized: I have zero passion in this stuff.

In 2019 my guiding question became: "how can I have more fun?"

Guess what I'm being guided to? More fun!

Each moment is a chance to ask a question that can open you up to what you want, or to what you don't want. If you're not intentionally choosing your questions, then you're letting yourself be guided by fears.

When you're sick if you ask, "when will this be over?" nothing helpful can come of it. When you ask "how can I feel better?" you may find yourself guided to certain teas or products that offer relief.

Try it now, ask yourself how you can experience something you want to experience. Like, "How can I welcome in more love?" or "How can I feel more peace?"

Get out your journal and jot down some questions you've caught yourself thinking today. No judgement, whatever you've been asking is fine.

Once you've done that, reword any that could be more helpful.

Choose your top question - the one that excites you the most - and gently close your eyes while breathing into this question. Be open. Be curious. And enjoy.

CHAPTER 19: ZONING OUT

I know it sounds like I'm asking you to constantly be mindful and do tons of work.

If you gotta zone out from time to time, I actually think there's a place for that too! Zoning out to an episode of your favorite show can be a useful tool.

Sometimes my emotions are too intense to lovingly embrace in the moment and I need to hit pause. This is when I'll take an intentional break.

I've practiced many ways of zoning out over the years. I'm very well-versed in avoidance and procrastination. I could run away from my feelings a million times before ever facing them.

That's not what I'm talking about in this chapter.

I used to binge and purge multiple times a day, watch twelve hours of television in a row that made me anxious when I should have been sleeping, use substances just to avoid feeling anything…

That's *not* intentional zoning out - that's self-destruction. Here's how to tell the difference: Is the activity you're using to zone out harmful? Does it make you feel better in the moment but worse in the long run? If either answer is yes, it's not something that fits into what I'm suggesting in this chapter. When we are our most heroic self, we have no need to self-destruct.

Now, instead, I intentionally indulge in something that makes me feel good both in the moment *and afterwards* and I give myself positive limits.

Instead of binge eating three dozen cookies, two large pizzas and a butterfinger bar before forcing myself to vomit, now instead I might indulge in ONE large slice of cake, vegan of course. And I'll take my time. I'll really let myself *enjoy every bite*. And I'll feel good about my body doing the work to fully digest it.

Or, instead of watching twelve hours of heart-pumping shows on Netflix that conveniently come with endless seasons for me to be unable to pull my eyes off of, I deliberately find and choose shows I can't get hooked on that make me feel better after watching them. For example, instead of being glued to an entire season of Arrow, I can simply watch one episode of The Office. Or three!

The difference here is that I'm giving myself boundaries that still allow me to indulge but in ways that don't make me feel crappy after.

Sometimes if I'm having a really hard day and I'm not ready yet to do the work of facing my emotions with love, I just need an hour or so of laughing at Michael Scott to take the edge off before sitting in meditation and working with my fears.

It's okay if occasional, intentional numbing out is part of your self-care plan as long as you can do it *responsibly.* And as long as you *know* you're doing it.

Too often we do it completely mindlessly. For example: scrolling through Instagram or watching YouTube video after YouTube video.

That's not to say I don't still do it, or that it's bad to do, but a lot of times when we're doing it it's because we're avoiding being alone with ourselves. We're avoiding feeling something. Or avoiding dealing with something.

It feels very different when you know you need to go F.U.N. Journal but you're just giving yourself permission first to go scroll through Bored Panda (my personal fave way to zone out online) or watch one episode of New Girl while eating a bowl of ice cream. Whatever you need to do to intentionally lift yourself up however slightly in that emotional spectrum from Chapter 10 is a good thing. The closer you get to neutral, the easier it is to do the work you gotta do to put those emotions to good use.

This advice doesn't apply to the crutches you use that you know you cannot just dabble in. In those cases it's about finding healthier substitutes. I want to point out, I said "healthier" - doesn't have to mean it's completely healthy. The more you make these subtle switches, the easier and easier it becomes to make healthier and healthier substitutes.

If you can indulge in numbing out but with intention, then you may want to consider making that part of your practice.

The only reason I'm putting it in here is that in my journey to finding stable, maintainable emotional health - no one gave me that permission. If you, like me, feel guilty for letting yourself do something slightly unhealthy when you're on a self-care mission, let this be the official permission you need that it actually *can* be part of a healthy lifestyle when done intentionally and lovingly.

CHAPTER 20: MAKE PEACE WITH YOUR PURPOSE BY KNOWING WHO YOU ARE

"I AM GROOT"
~Groot

Be honest.

How much of your anxiety comes from not knowing what you want to do with your life or wondering if you're living life the "right way"?

It makes sense! You are a passionate person. People lacking strong passions don't tend to experience those same concerns.

Perhaps you've already uncovered during your F.U.N. journaling that this is a specific hotpoint for you.

That's great! If you experience a lot of emotions below neutral when it comes to thinking about your purpose, that's an exciting place to be.

It means your purpose is very important to you and you likely do not want to live what most would consider an ordinary life.

For many, purpose is synonymous with career.

We often think that our purpose revolves around our job, our family or whatever other role we play.

It's much simpler than that.

YOU are you're purpose.

Being the truest *you* you can be - what greater purpose *is* there? Literally no one else can fulfill that purpose besides you.

It's not about the job, the grades, the recognition. Yes, of course, you want to make sure your career aligns with something you feel good about, but never mistake that for your purpose.

You can't get your purpose wrong when you are living each day in gratitude as yourself.

If you show up as you, you're doing it right my friend.

It's time to make peace with this and accept it. You cannot get it wrong.

And the beauty is that the truer you are to you, the more everything around you (career included) begins to line up with your deepest passions and desires - but that's *secondary.* First you must accept that to live your purpose, you just must live as you.

Not the person others want or need you to be.

The person you feel you are deep inside.

Aligning with the you-est version of you is the greatest gift you could give yourself.

Get out your journal and answer these questions. You don't have to know the right answers. Whatever you answer is right *in this moment.* These answers will change and grow and develop as you do. For now, just free right whatever responses come to mind. If nothing comes to mind, skip it and be open. When you're struck by inspiration come back to it. Everything comes to us in perfect timing, including answers.

Journal questions:
What lights me up?
What do I stand for?
How do I want others to feel when they're in my presence?
How do I feel when I'm true to myself?
Who am I really?

CHAPTER 21: WEAR THE CAPE

Take a moment to be proud of all the work you've done so far. We're almost done, but before we get to the finish line, just take a moment to reflect.

Being gifted with intensity is a big responsibility, as we've discussed.

You have to go through a lot that not everyone does. Even if you're not being put through actual physical harm or danger, you may often be struggling with challenges that feel very significant.

When this happens we often tend to want to act a certain way to hide it or make it seem like everything is okay.

Everything is okay because there's nothing wrong with feeling terrible!

There is nothing to hide. No reason to put on a mask

and act like everything is okay. Wear the cape, not the mask.

To put on your cape is to *own* every emotion and wear it with pride. There is nothing wrong with anything you feel.

> *To be a superhero is to be uniquely, truly and honestly you. To own every feeling. To use your feelings to better your life. To better your life so that you can better serve.*

So, do you want to wear the cape?

Do the work to truly feel. Be accepting of every emotion and set the example for others to do the same.

It is heroic to feel all our feels.

That, my friend, is how you wear your cape.

If you're committed, move forward into the next steps to truly launch you forward into the superhero that you are.

Journal Reflection:
How did I feel about my emotions under neutral when I started this?
How do I feel about them now?
In what ways am I ready to show up in the world as the hero version of myself?
In what ways have I changed since starting this process?

CHAPTER 22: THE MANIFESTO

Holy smokes, here we are.

The grand finale.

This is the most powerful tool of 'em all, baby!

But it's last for a good reason. If you're not doing the rest of work, this is pretty useless.

You now know that you create your reality.

You now know that your fears are of service.

You now know that it's safe to love and accept every emotion you feel.

Now it's time to create your **hero manifesto** to help you move forward. This will be a living document designed to guide you.

I created one that guides my life and I'm excited for you to create yours. All you gotta do is use this process:

Get out your journal. Find a quiet, private space. If you can, prepare yourself by lighting a candle or setting an intention. This is a special process you're doing, so treat it that way.

Before you start take about ten to fifteen minutes to sit and focus on your breath. Any time a thought emerges, that's okay, just return to your breath. Eventually you will reach this really quiet space in your mind. Once you have a few moments in that headspace, start answering these questions:

1. Who am I?
2. What do I stand for?
3. How do I want to make people feel?
4. What do I *want* to believe?
5. How do I want to live?
6. What steps do I take to live this way?

That's it.

Six simple questions with profound results.

Once you have this manifesto, go type it up, turn it into a poster, put it somewhere you can read it often. When you find yourself slipping on the beliefs you desire to have or the way you desire to live your life, return to this. If you find your answers changing over time, update them. It's okay to evolve!

Every hero has a mission. This is yours. I am forever

Marisa Imon

grateful to you.

CHAPTER 23: GO FORTH AND PROSPER

All superheroes must continue to put their hard work and dedication into action every single day to stay heroic. You are no different.

What you've learned in this book needs to be continuously practiced to strengthen your ability to use your emotional intensity for good.

Each day moving forward commit to:
- Practicing a morning and evening routine that feels right to you (Chapter 17)
- F.U.N. journaling about any emotions that are below neutral to change your beliefs. Do this with at least one feeling daily. (Chapter 10)
- Writing or mentally creating gratitude lists
- Lovingly accepting of all your emotions
- Listening to your intuition
- Reading your manifesto
- Sleeping

It's not a huge amount of things to commit to really.

And you're more than capable.

Thank you for being on this journey together. If you haven't already signed up for my **free weekly meditations designed to bring out the superhero in you**, head over to my website, www.marisaimon.com now to continue this journey.

I am so excited for you. Thank you for showing up, hero.

△△△

Made in the
USA
Middletown, DE